PIANO • VOCAL

BROADWAY MUSICALS
Show by Show
1930-1939

blic

D0520246

CONTENTS

HAL•LEONARD®
CORPORATION

7777 W. BLUEMOUND RD. P.O. BOX 13819 MILWAUKEE, WI 53213

ISBN 0-7935-0779-0

Foreword

The Broadway musical, with its combination of music, dancing and visual delights, is truly one of America's great cultural treasures. From the hundreds of productions which have been mounted since 1891, we've selected the best music, and combined it with interesting facts and photographs to create a one-of-a-kind seven-volume songbook series: Broadway Musicals - Show By Show.

About The Author Of The Text

The comments about each show in this collection are excerpted from the book *Broadway Musicals Show by Show* by author Stanley Green. Mr. Green (1923-1990) was highly regarded as one of the leading scholars in the field of musical theatre. His eleven books are among the most widely read on the subject, including *The World of Musical Comedy, The Rodgers and Hammerstein Story, Broadway Musicals of the 30s, Starring Fred Astaire, Encyclopaedia of the Musical Theatre, Encyclopaedia of the Musical Film, The Great Clowns of Broadway, Broadway Musicals Show by Show,* and *Hollywood Musicals Year by Year.* He also compiled and edited *The Rodgers and Hammerstein Fact Book,* the definitive reference on that phenomenally successful collaboration.

Mr. Green was born in New York and lived there throughout his life. He began his writing career as a record reviewer for *Saturday Review,* and later was a contributing editor for *HiFi/Stereo Review.* His articles appeared regularly in such publications as *The New York Times, Musical America, Variety,* and *The Atlantic Monthly.* He worked as a film publicist in New York and London, and was public relations advisor to ASCAP for the years 1961-1965. In 1967 he wrote the script for the revue *Salute to the American Musical Theatre,* first performed at the Waldorf-Astoria, and subsequently presented at the White House on three consecutive evenings. He also wrote the script for "The Music of Kurt Weill" and was music advisor for "Review of Reviews," two programs presented at Lincoln Center in New York.

In 1974, at the request of Richard Rodgers, Mr. Green appeared with the composer on the first videotaped program for the Theatre Collection of the New York Public Library at Lincoln Center. He has been involved with many recording projects, including a 100-record series on Broadway musicals for the Franklin Mint, and the album *Starring Fred Astaire,* which he co-produced for Columbia. In 1987 he moderated a series of seminars marking the 100th birthday of George Abbott. Mr. Green presented many lectures on musical theatre and film at Union College, University of Hartford, New York University, C. W. Post College, Lincoln Center Library, Goodspeed Opera, and Marymount College. He continued to be active as a writer and researcher until the time of his death in December of 1990.

STRIKE UP THE BAND

Music:
George Gershwin

Lyrics:
Ira Gershwin

Book:
Morrie Ryskind

Producer:
Edgar Selwyn

Director:
Alexander Leftwich

Choreographer:
George Hale

Cast:
Bobby Clark & Paul McCullough,
Blanche Ring, Jerry Goff,
Doris Carson, Dudley Clements,
Red Nichols Orchestra

Songs:
"I Mean to Say";
"Soon"; "Strike Up the Band";
Mademoiselle in New Rochelle";
I've Got a Crush on You"

New York run:
Times Square Theatre,
January 14, 1930; 191 p.

*S*trike Up the Band was first scheduled for a Broadway opening in 1927, but the original George S. Kaufman book was so uncompromisingly grim in its antiwar sentiment that the show closed on the road. Morrie Ryskind then rewrote the story, putting most of the action in a dream, and the leading roles were given to the zany team of Clark and McCullough. The revised script dealt with a war between the United States and Switzerland over the issue of tariffs on imported Swiss chocolate, with plenty of room for barbs aimed at jingoists, politicians, and White House advisers. Musical-comedy conventions, however, helped make it palatable to 1930 audiences. This was the first of a number of book shows and revues of the Thirties that, influenced by the Depression and the growing threat of another World War, were emboldened to make satirical observations on the problems then besetting the country and the world. Of interest to jazz buffs is that Red Nichols' pit band included such future luminaries as Benny Goodman, Gene Krupa, Glenn Miller, Jimmy Dorsey and Jack Teagarden.

FINE AND DANDY

Music: Kay Swift

Lyrics: Paul James

Book: Donald Ogden Stewart
(Joe Cook uncredited)

Producers: Morris Green & Lewis Gensler

Directors: Morris Green, Frank McCoy

Choreographers: David Gould, Tom Nip

Cast:
Joe Cook, Nell O'Day, Dave Chasen, Eleanor
Powell, Alice Boulden, Joe Wagstaff

Songs:
"Fine and Dandy"; "Can This Be Love?"; "Let's
Go Eat Worms in the Garden"; "The Jig Hop"

New York run:
Erlanger's Theatre, September 23, 1930; 255 p.

*C*omic Joe Cook was an innocent looking clown with a wide smile whose specialties were non sequitur stories (including his trademark routine about why he would not imitate four Hawaiians), Rube Goldberg-type inventions, and acrobatic and juggling skills. *Fine and Dandy,* a follow-up to his popular vehicle, *Rain or Shine,* not only included the Cook specialties but also featured a superior score (including the durable title song), the tapping of Eleanor Powell, and a tale that found Cook as Joe Squibb, the general manager of the Fordyce Drop Forge and Tool Factory, who ineptly copes with problems of labor and management. Erlanger's Theatre, now the St. James, stands on 44th Street west of Broadway.

GIRL CRAZY

Music: George Gershwin

Lyrics: Ira Gershwin

Book: Guy Bolton & John McGowan

Producers: Alex A. Aarons & Vinton Freedley

Director: Alexander Leftwich

Choreographer: George Hale

Cast:
Willie Howard, Allen Kearns, Ginger Rogers,
William Kent, Ethel Merman, Antonio & Renee
DeMarco, Lew Parker, Roger Edens, Red
Nichols Orchestra

Songs:
"Bidin' My Time";
"Could You Use Me?"; "Embraceable You"; "I
Got Rhythm"; "But Not for Me"; "
Sam and Delilah"; "Treat Me Rough"

New York run:
Alvin Theatre, October 14, 1930; 272 p.

*T*emporarily turning from the satiric world of their recent *Strike Up the Band*, the Gershwin brothers joined their former colleagues, librettist Guy Bolton and producers Aarons and Freedley, to escape to the more innocent world of conventional musical comedy. For *Girl Crazy*, however, they abandoned the East Coast haunts of high society that had been their customary locales in favor of the wide open spaces of Custerville, Arizona. There playboy Danny Churchill (Allen Kearns) has been sent by his wealthy father to manage a ranch in order to keep out of the clutches of predatory females. Arriving by taxi from New York, Danny soon turns the place into a dude ranch where Kate Fothergill (Ethel Merman in her first Broadway role) entertains guests with the undeniable assertion, "I Got Rhythm." Later our hero gets to croon "Embraceable You" with Molly Gray (Ginger Rogers in her second Broadway role), and helps taxi driver-turned-sheriff Gieber Goldfarb (Willie Howard in a part intended for Bert Lahr) apprehend the outlaw who has been threatening his life. Red Nichols' band included the same impressive personnel as in *Strike Up the Band*. Three film adaptations were made of *Girl Crazy*, with Judy Garland and Mickey Rooney co-starred in the 1943 version.

THE NEW YORKERS

Music & lyrics: Cole Porter

Book: Herbert Fields

Producer: E. Ray Goetz

Director: Monty Woolley

Choreographer: George Hale

Cast:
Frances Williams, Charles King,
Hope Williams, Ann Pennington, Richard
Carle, Marie Cahill, Fred Waring Orchestra,
Clayton, Jackson and Durante, Kathryn
Crawford, Oscar Ragland

Songs:
"Where Have You Been?"; "Love for Sale";
"Take Me Back to Manhattan"; "Let's Fly
Away"; "I Happen to Like New York"

New York run:
Broadway Theatre, December 8, 1930; 168 p.

*T*he first stage production at the Broadway Theatre (on 53rd Street), *The New Yorkers* was something of a forerunner of *Pal Joey* in its amoral characters, cynical outlook and flashy nightclub atmosphere. Just as Cole Porter and Herbert Fields' previous *Fifty Million Frenchmen* had offered a musical tour of Paris, so the new outing (with the same producer and director) offered a musical tour of high and low life in Manhattan, stopping off at a Park Avenue apartment, a speak-easy, a bootleg distillery, the Cotton Club in Harlem and Reuben's Restaurant on Madison Avenue. The surrealistic satire concerns a socialite (Hope Williams) in love with a bootlegger (Charles King) because she is impressed with the way he bumps people off. Other characters include the lady's philandering parents and an irrepressible gangster henchman (Jimmy Durante), who brings the first act to a riotous close with his description of the varied products made from wood. Soon after the show's opening, Elisabeth Welch replaced Kathryn Crawford to sing the torchy invitation of a streetwalker, "Love for Sale."

THREE'S A CROWD

Music:
Arthur Schwartz, etc.

Lyrics:
Howard Dietz, etc.

Sketches:
Miscellaneous writers

Producer:
Max Gordon

Director:
Hassard Short

Choreographer:
Albertina Rasch

Cast:
Clifton Webb, Fred Allen, Libby Holman,
Tamara Geva, Portland Hoffa, Earl Oxford,
Fred MacMurray

Songs:
"Something to Remember You By"; "Body and
Soul" (Johnny Green-Edward Heyman, Robert
Sour); "The Moment I Saw You"; "Forget All
Your Books" (music: Burton Lane); "Right at
the Start of It"

New York run:
Selwyn Theatre, October 15, 1930; 272 p.

Three's A Crowd. Libby Holman singing "Something to Remember You By" as she bids farewell to matelot Fred MacMurray. (Apeda)

*O*nce the sponsors of *The Second Little Show* decided that the stars of the first *Little Show* — Clifton Webb, Fred Allen, and Libby Holman — would not be in their new revue, fledgling producer Max Gordon persuaded the trio to appear in his own revue. He further assured that *Three's a Crowd* would be accepted in fact if not in name as the sequel to *The Little Show* by bringing along composer Arthur Schwartz and lyricist Howard Dietz (with Dietz additionally credited with having "conceived and compiled" the new show). The musical standouts of the evening were Miss Holman's masochistic "Body and Soul" and her "Something to Remember You By," a tearful ballad of farewell she sang to a matelot played by Fred MacMurray. Fred Allen won his biggest laughs as explorer Admiral Byrd, who has just returned from the Antarctic to announce his discovery of 500,000 square miles of brand new snow.

THE BAND WAGON

Music:
Arthur Schwartz

Lyrics:
Howard Dietz

Sketches:
George S. Kaufman, Howard Dietz

Producer:
Max Gordon

Director:
Hassard Short

Choreographer:
Albertina Rasch

Cast:
Fred & Adele Astaire,
Frank Morgan,
Helen Broderick,
Tilly Losch,
Philip Loeb,
John Barker

Songs:
"Sweet Music";
"High and Low";
"Hoops"; "Confession";
"New Sun in the Sky";
"I Love Louisa";
"Dancing in the Dark";
"White Heat"

New York run:
New Amsterdam Theatre, June 3, 1931; 260 p.

The Band Wagon. "The Pride of the Claghornes" sketch with Helen Broderick, Adele Astaire, Frank Morgan, and Fred Astaire. (Vandamm)

*P*ut together by the same creative team that had been responsible for *Three's a Crowd, The Band Wagon* may well have been the most sophisticated, imaginative, and musically distinguished revue ever mounted on Broadway. To assure that the production would have the same homogeneity of style as a book musical, there were no interpolations in the score and only two writers were credited for the sketches. Among the evening's pleasures Fred and Adele Astaire (in their tenth and last Broadway appearance together) as two French children cavorting to "Hoops"; the principals riding on a Bavarian merry-go-round while singing "I Love Louisa"; Tilly Losch dancing to "Dancing in the Dark" on a slanted, mirrored stage; "The Pride of the Claghornes" sketch spoofing the Southern aristocracy's honor-of-the-family code. *The Band Wagon* was also the first New York production to use a double revolving stage for both its musical numbers and sketches. The 1953 Fred Astaire-Cyd Charisse film retained five songs, added others, and threw in a story line.

Cover designed by John Held, Jr.

The Band Wagon. Adele and Fred Astaire singing "Hoops." (Vandamm)

OF THEE I SING

Music: George Gershwin

Lyrics: Ira Gershwin

Book: George S. Kaufman & Morrie Ryskind

Producer: Sam H. Harris

Director: George S. Kaufman

Choreographer: George Hale

Cast:
William Gaxton,
Victor Moore,
Lois Moran,
Grace Brinkley,
June O'Dea,
George Murphy,
Dudley Clements,
Edward H. Robins,
Florenz Ames,
Ralph Riggs,
George E. Mack

Songs:
"Wintergreen for President";
"Because, Because";
"Love Is Sweeping the Country";
"Of Thee I Sing, Baby";
"Here's a Kiss for Cinderella"; "Who Cares?";
"Hello, Good Morning";
"The Illegitimate Daughter"

New York run:
Music Box, December 26, 1931; 441 p.

Of Thee I Sing. Victor Moore and William Gaxton, surrounded by political advisers, getting ready for the campaign. (Vandamm)

*C*onstructed more in the style of a Gilbert and Sullivan comic opera than of a Broadway musical comedy, *Of Thee I Sing* was an extension of the satirical approach of the same writers' previous *Strike Up The Band.* Here, however, the technique was surer and the compromises to popular taste less apparent, with songs and story complementing each other and expressing a uniform point of view. Sharply and deftly skewered were such institutions as political conventions and campaigns, beauty pageants, marriage, the Vice Presidency, the Supreme Court, foreign affairs and motherhood.

The fanciful tale covers the fortunes of the Presidential ticket of John P. Wintergreen and his running mate, Alexander Throttlebottom — abetted by Wintergreen's bride, Mary Turner (Lois Moran) — which, with its campaign song "Of Thee I Sing, Baby," sweeps the country on a platform of Love. Once in office, however, the President is threatened with impeachment because he jilted Diana Devereaux (Grace Brinkley), the Miss America contest winner he had promised to marry. She, it seems, is "the illegitimate daughter of the illegitimate son of an illegitimate nephew of Napoleon," and France is insulted because of this slight. After the First Lady somehow saves the day by giving birth to twins, France's honor is assuaged when Throttlebottom agrees to wed Diana because, according to the Constitution, "When the President of the United States is unable to fulfill his duties, his obligations are assumed by the Vice President."

Of The I Sing, the third longest running musical of the Thirties, became the first musical ever awarded the Pulitzer Prize for drama (though ironically George Gershwin was not included in the citation since his was a musical contribution and therefore not considered eligible for a literary award). It also established brash, sharp-featured William Gaxton and bumbling, dumpling-shaped Victor Moore, who played Wintergreen and Throttlebottom, as Broadway's leading musical-comedy team. After touring, the show returned to New York for a month-long engagement in May 1933. It then resumed its tour with a cast headed by Oscar Shaw, Donald Meek, and Ann Sothern.

In October 1933, a sequel, *Let 'Em Eat Cake,* written by the same writers and featuring the original leading players, opened on Broadway. Supposedly a satire on dictatorship, the show proved too acerbic and thematically confusing, and it remained only three months. The Song "Mine," which was in this production, was added to *Of Thee I Sing* when the musical was revived in 1952. Jack Carson and Victor Moore were signed to play Wintergreen and Throttlebottom, but Moore decided against repeating his original role and the part went to Paul Hartman. George S. Kaufman again directed. In 1987, a concert version was performed with *Let 'Em Eat Cake* at the Brooklyn Academy of Music.

THE CAT AND THE FIDDLE

Music:
Jerome Kern

Lyrics & book:
Otto Harbach

Producer:
Max Gordon

Director:
José Ruben

Choreographer:
Albertina Rasch

Cast:
Georges Metaxa,
Bettina Hall, Odette Myrtil,
Eddie Foy Jr., José Ruben,
Lawrence Grossmith, Doris Carson,
George Meader

Songs:
"The Night Was Made for Love";
"I Watch the Love Parade"; "Try to Forget";
"Poor Pierrot"; "She Didn't Say 'Yes'";
"A New Love Is Old"; "One Moment Alone"

New York run:
Globe Theatre, October 15, 1931; 395 p.

The Cat and the Fiddle. Georges Metaxa, George Meader, and Bettina Hall. (White)

*T*he Cat and the Fiddle was a generally successful attempt to put the florid operetta form into a contemporary, intimate setting. In creating the work, Jerome Kern and Otto Harbach did without choruses, spectacles, and dragged-in comedy routines to keep the focus on the main story of what they called "A Musical Romance." Set in modern Brussels, it tells of the attraction between Victor Florescu (Georges Metaxa), a serious-minded Rumanian composer, and Shirley Sheridan (Bettina Hall), a vivacious American composer with a penchant for jazz. Though Victor is furious when a producer tries to lighten his rather heavy operetta, *The Passionate Pilgrim,* with some of Shirley's bright, uptempo numbers, true love eventually has hero and heroine singing in harmony. The true hero of the evening, however, was Jerome Kern whose score was an almost continuous flow of melodic pleasures, with songs well integrated into the story and with a highly advanced use of musical underscoring. In 1934, a film version was released starring Jeanette MacDonald and Ramon Novarro.

GEORGE WHITE'S SCANDALS

Music: Ray Henderson

Lyrics: Lew Brown

Sketches:
Lew Brown, George White, Irving Caesar

Producer-director-choreographer:
George White

Cast:
Rudy Vallee, Ethel Merman, Willie &
Eugene Howard, Everett Marshall, Ray Bolger,
Ethel Barrymore Colt, Alice Faye

Songs:
"Life Is Just a Bowl of Cherries";
"The Thrill Is Gone"; "This Is the Misus";
"Ladies and Gentlemen, That's Love";
"That's Why Darkies Were Born"; "My Song"

New York run:
Apollo Theatre, September 14, 1931; 202 p.

*T*he only challenger to the 1926 *Scandals* (see page 52) as the best of the series was the 11th Edition, which came along in 1931. Ray Henderson and Lew Brown (but minus B. G. DeSylva) were on hand for their fourth and last *Scandals* together with an impressive array of song hits introduced by pop crooner Rudy Vallee, powerhouse belter Ethel Merman (who had joined the cast during the tryout), and robust baritone Everett Marshall. Among the attractions were a celebration of the opening of the Empire State Building with Ray Bolger as a dancing Al Smith (with decor by former Ziegfeld designer Joseph Urban); a chins-up Depression anthem, "Life Is Just a Bowl of Cherries," trumpeted by Miss Merman; Willie and Eugene Howard in their classic comedy sketch "Pay the Two Dollars"; and a bold first-act finale, "That's Why Darkies Were Born," that took a compassionate view of Negro fortitude in the face of injustice.

FACE THE MUSIC

Music & lyrics: Irving Berlin

Book: Moss Hart

Producer: Sam H. Harris

Directors: Hassard Short, George S. Kaufman

Choreographer: Albertina Rasch

Cast:
Mary Boland, J. Harold Murray, Andrew Tombes, Hugh O'Connell, Katherine Carrington, David Burns

Songs:
"Let's Have Another Cup o' Coffee";
"On a Roof in Manhattan"; "Soft Lights and Sweet Music"; "I Say It's Spinach"

New York run:
New Amsterdam Theatre,
February 17, 1932; 165 p.

*T*he mood of cynicism created by the Depression continued to spawn a number of sharply satirical Broadway musicals. The Gershwin brothers George S. Kaufman and Morrie Ryskind had led the way with *Strike Up the Band* and *Of Thee I Sing,* and now it was the turn of Irving Berlin and Moss Hart (with Kaufman joining the project as director). In *Face the Music* the concern was with New York politicians and policemen with little tin boxes the reduced financial circumstances of the city's elite (former wealthy socialites sing "Let's Have Another Cup o' Coffee" in the Automat) and the insane world of the theatre. In the leading role Mary Boland played Mrs. Martin Van Buren Meshbesher, the wife of a police sergeant "lousy with money," who tries to lose some of it by backing a tasteless Broadway show, *The Rhinestone Girl,* that surprisingly becomes a hit. Despite the Seabury investigation into police corruption (which also figured in the 1959 musical, *Fiorello!),* the boys in blue manage to beat the rap when Mrs. Meshbesher contributes the profits from the show to the city's depleted treasury. Early in 1933 *Face the Music* returned to Broadway for a month-long run.

GAY DIVORCE

Music & lyrics:
Cole Porter

Book:
Dwight Taylor

Producers:
Dwight Deere Wiman & Tom Weatherly

Director:
Howard Lindsay

Choreographers:
Carl Randall, Barbara Newberry

Cast:
Fred Astaire, Claire Luce, Luella Gear, Betty Starbuck, Erik Rhodes, Eric Blore, G. P. Huntley Jr.

Songs:
"After You, Who?";
"Night and Day";
"How's Your Romance?";
"I've Got You on My Mind";
"Mister and Missus Fitch"

New York run:
Ethel Barrymore Theatre,
November 29, 1932; 248 p.

*T*he first musical to play the Ethel Barrymore Theatre (on 47th Street west of Broadway), *Gay Divorce* was the only stage production in which Fred Astaire performed without sister Adele. In the story, adapted from an unproduced play, Astaire was seen as Guy Holden, a British novelist, who goes to a seaside resort to woo would-be divorcée Mimi Pratt (Claire Luce), primarily by convincing her — through song and dance — that night and day she is the one. Complications arise when Guy is mistaken for a professional corespondent (Erik Rhodes) who has been hired to ease Mimi s divorce. Though Astaire proved that he could carry both a weak plot and a new dancing partner, *Gay Divorce* (without the definite article, please) marked his final appearance on Broadway. The 1934 film version, retitled *The Gay Divorcee,* co-starred Fred with Ginger Rogers.

MUSIC IN THE AIR

Music:
Jerome Kern

Lyrics & book:
Oscar Hammerstein II

Producer:
Peggy Fears
(A. C. Blumenthal uncredited)

Directors:
Jerome Kern & Oscar Hammerstein II

Cast:
Reinald Werrenrath, Natalie Hall,
Tullio Carminati, Katherine Carrington,
Al Shean, Walter Slezak,
Nicholas Joy, Marjorie Main

Songs:
"I've Told Ev'ry Little Star";
"There's a Hill Beyond a Hill";
"And Love Was Born";
"I'm Alone";
"I Am So Eager";
"One More Dance";
"When the Spring Is in the Air";
"In Egern on the Tegern See";
"The Song Is You";
"We Belong Together"

New York run:
Alvin Theatre, November 8, 1932; 342 p.

Music In The Air. Katherine Carrington, Al Shean and Walter Slezak. (Vandamm)

*H*ailed by Alexander Woollcott in *The New Yorker as* "that endearing refuge, that gracious shelter from a troubled world," the Jerome Kern-Oscar Hammerstein *Music in* the Air continued along the same path as the Jerome Kern-Otto Harbach *Cat and the Fiddle.* The setting was again modern Europe, the story again had to do with the preparations for an operetta, and the songs — among Kern's most memorable — and the underscoring again enhanced the characters and the situations. The plot of this "Musical Adventure" concerns Sieglinde and Karl (Katherine Carrington and Walter Slezak), two Bavarian naifs, who hike from Edendorf to Munich to help Sieglinde's father, Dr. Walther Lessing (Al Shean), interest a music publisher in his new composition, "I've Told Ev'ry Little Star." Soon they become involved with glamorous star Frieda Hatzfeld (Natalie Hall) and her lover, librettist Bruno Mahler (Tullio Carminati), during the rehearsals of Bruno's new work, *Tingle-Tangle.* When the temperamental diva walks out on the production, Sieglinde is given her big chance. Contrary to show-business legend, however, she proves totally inept, and when Frieda comes back Sieglinde sadly returns to her mountain village.

Hammerstein brought Music in the Air back to Broadway in 1951, with a cast headed by Jane Pickens (Frieda), Dennis King (Bruno), and Charles Winninger (Lessing). Because of possible anti-German sentiment following World War II, he changed the locale from Munich to Zurich and made everybody Swiss. The show remained less than two months. The 1934 Hollywood version starred Gloria Swanson, John Boles, and Al Shean.

TAKE A CHANCE

Music:
Richard A. Whiting,
Nacio Herb Brown,
Vincent Youmans

Lyrics:
B. G. DeSylva

Book:
B. G. DeSylva,
Laurence Schwab,
Sid Silvers

Producer:
Laurence Schwab & B. G. DeSylva

Director:
Edgar MacGregor

Choreographer:
Bobby Connolly

Cast:
Jack Haley, Ethel Merman, Jack Whiting,
Sid Silvers, June Knight, Mitzi Mayfair,
Oscar Ragland, Robert Gleckler

Songs:
"Should I Be Sweet?" (Youmans);
"Turn Out the Lights" (Whiting, Brown);
"Rise 'n' Shine" (Youmans);
"You're an Old Smoothie" (Whiting, Brown);
"Eadie Was a Lady" (Whiting; lyric with
Roger Edens)

New York run:
Apollo Theatre, November 26, 1932; 243 p.

*I*n September 1932, a musical titled *Humpty Dumpty* began its tryout tour in Pittsburgh. It involved Lou Holtz, Ethel Merman, and Eddie Foy Jr. in what was basically a revue with songs and sketches dealing with incidents in American history. It was so poorly received that the show closed in five days. Within three weeks however, the production was totally revised, partly recast (Holtz and Foy were replaced by Jack Whiting and Jack Haley), and had five new songs by Vincent Youmans. Retitled *Take a Chance* — to indicate something of the risks involved — the show was now an old-fashioned book musical concerned with a romance between the leading man and leading lady (Whiting and June Knight) who are appearing in a revue about American history called *Humpty Dumpty*. What turned it into a hit, though, were the comedy and specialty numbers, with Miss Merman given two show stoppers — "Rise 'n' Shine" and "Eadie Was a Lady" — that let her blast her way clear up to the second balcony. During the Broadway run, Haley and Sid Silvers were succeeded by the vaudeville team of Olsen and Johnson. The film version, released in 1933, featured June Knight and Lillian Roth.

FLYING COLORS

Music:
Arthur Schwartz

Lyrics & sketches:
Howard Dietz

Producer:
Max Gordon

Director:
Howard Dietz

Choreographer:
Albertina Rasch

Cast:
**Clifton Webb, Charles Butterworth,
Tamara Geva, Patsy Kelly, Philip Loeb,
Vilma & Buddy Ebsen, Larry Adler,
Imogene Coca, Monette Moore**

Songs:
**"Two-Faced Woman";
"A Rainy Day";
"A Shine on Your Shoes";
"Alone Together";
"Louisiana Hayride";
"Smokin' Reefers"**

New York run:
Imperial Theatre, September 15, 1932, 188 p.

Flying Colors. Buddy Ebsen, Monette Moore, Vilma Ebsen, and Larry Adler performing "A Shine on Your Shoes." (White)

*F*lying *Colors* flew in a direct line from *The Little Show, Three's a Crowd*, and *The Band Wagon*. Like all three, it had music by Arthur Schwark and lyrics by Howard Dietz (though this time Dietz also received credit as sole sketch writer and director). Like the most recent two revues, it was produced by Max Gordon and was choreographed by Albertina Rasch, and it also featured two veterans of the series, Clifton Webb and Tamara Geva. Though too closely patterned after its illustrious predecessors (Brooks Atkinson headed his Sunday *Times* piece, "Flying the Band Wagon Colors"), the show was witty and attractive, and had its share of standout numbers: "A Shine on Your Shoes" presented Vilma and Buddy Ebsen dancing around a shoeshine stand accompanied by Larry Adler's harmonica; "Alone Together" offered Webb and Geva in a dramatic, sinuous dance; and "Louisiana Hayride" brought the first act to a jubilant close. Then there was Charles Butterworth's hilarious soapbox speech, "Harvey Woofter's Five Point Plan," on how to end the Depression. Times were tough for the show, too. After opening it at a $4.40 top, Gordon was soon forced to lower the ticket price to $2.20.

AS THOUSANDS CHEER

Music & lyrics:
Irving Berlin

Sketches:
Moss Hart

Producer:
Sam H. Harris

Director:
Hassard Short

Choreographer:
Charles Weidman

Cast:
**Marilyn Miller, Clifton Webb,
Helen Broderick, Ethel Waters,
Hal Forde, Jerome Cowan,
Harry Stockwell, José Limon, Letitia Ide,
Thomas Hamilton, Leslie Adams**

Songs:
**"How's Chances?";
"Heat Wave";
"Lonely Heart";
"Easter Parade";
"Supper Time";
"Harlem on My Mind";
"Not for All the Rice in China"**

New York run:
Music Box, September 30, 1933; 400 p.

As Thousands Cheer. King George V (Leslie Adams) and Queen Mary (Helen Broderick) are upset to read of the latest romantic escapade involving the Prince of Wales (Thomas Hamilton). (Vandamm)

*T*hough it was a revue, the Irving Berlin-Moss Hart *As Thousands Cheer* was considered a successor to the Berlin-Hart book musical, *Face the Music,* since it also dealt satirically with topics of current interest. In fact, it was so concerned with topicality that the entire show was structured in the form of a newspaper, with various stories and features — each one preceded by a blowup of a headline — depicted in songs, dances and sketches. In addition to general news, there were sections devoted to comics, rotogravure (an opportunity to show the Easter Parade of half a century earlier), society, theatre, the weather report ("Heat Wave") and advice to the lovelorn ("Lonely Heart"). As might be expected in a lighthearted entertainment, serious topics were avoided except for Ethel Waters' purposely jarring "Supper Time," introduced by the headline "UNKNOWN NEGRO LYNCHED BY FRENZIED MOB." Newsworthy individuals impersonated in the noteworthy show were Barbara Hutton and Joan Crawford (by Marilyn Miller in her 12th and final Broadway appearance); Douglas Fairbanks Jr., John D. Rockefeller, and Mahatma Gandhi (by Clifton Webb); Louise Hoover, Aimee Semple MacPherson, Queen Mary and the Statue of Liberty (by Helen Broderick); and Josephine Baker (by Miss Waters).

ROBERTA

Music:
Jerome Kern

Lyrics & book:
Otto Harbach

Producer:
Max Gordon

Director:
(Hassard Short uncredited)

Choreographer:
José Limon (John Lonergan uncredited)

Cast:
Lyda Roberti, Bob Hope,
Fay Templeton, Tamara,
George Murphy, Sydney Greenstreet,
Ray Middleton, Fred MacMurray

Songs:
"Let's Begin";
"You're Devastating";
"Yesterdays";
"The Touch of Your Hand";
"I'll Be Hard to Handle" (lyric: Bernard Dougall);
"Smoke Gets in Your Eyes";
"Something Had to Happen"

New York run:
New Amsterdam Theatre,
November 18, 1933; 295 p.

Roberta. Bob Hope catches Lyda Roberti and Ray Middleton in an embarrassing situation. (Vandamm)

*B*ased on Alice Duer Miller's popular novel, *Gowns by Roberta* (the original title was still used during the tryout), the production was expected to follow *The Cat and the Fiddle* and *Music in the Air* as another of Jerome Kern's well-intergrated modern operettas set in present-day Europe. The work, however, turned out to be more of a formula musical comedy dependent upon sumptuously mounted production numbers (one was a fashion show), some comic interpolations, and a superior collection of songs — including "Smoke Gets in Your Eyes" and "Yesterdays" — that bore little relevance to the plot. Said plot had to do with a former All-American fullback, John Kent (Ray Middleton), who inherits a Paris dress salon owned by his Aunt Minnie (Fay Templeton). John also ends with Minnie's assistant, Russian Princess Stephanie (Tamara), as both business and marital partner. Bob Hope, in his first major Broadway role, played John's band leader chum, Huckleberry Haines. Though *Roberta* was initially directed by Kern himself, the composer was replaced by the more experienced Hassard Short who refused program credit. In 1935, the first of two screen versions co-starred Irene Dunne, Fred Astaire and Ginger Rogers.

ZIEGFELD FOLLIES

Music:
Vernon Duke, etc.

Lyrics:
E. Y. Harburg, etc.

Sketches:
Miscellaneous writers

Producer:
Billie Burke Ziegfeld
(Messrs. Shubert uncredited)

Directors:
Bobby Connolly, Edward Clark Lilley,
John Murray Anderson

Choreographers:
Bobby Connolly, Robert Alton

Cast:
Fanny Brice, Willie & Eugene Howard,
Everett Marshall, Jane Froman,
Vilma & Buddy Ebsen, Patricia Bowman,
Cherry & June Preisser, Eve Arden,
Robert Cummings, Ina Ray Hutton

Songs:
"I Like the Likes of You";
"Suddenly";
"What Is There to Say?";
"The Last Round-Up" (Billy Hill);
"Wagon Wheels" (Peter DeRose-Hill)

New York run:
Winter Garden, January 4, 1934; 182 p.

Ziegfeld Follies. Willie Howard and Fanny Brice in the sketch based on *Sailor, Beware!*

*I*n the mid-Thirties the Shubert brothers offered five revues at the Winter Garden that won general approval for their high level of comedy, inventive staging, attractive decor, and musical quality. The first of these, the 1934 *Ziegfeld Follies,* had begun its tryout tour so unpromisingly, however, that director John Murray Anderson and choreographer Robert Alton were rushed in to replace Bobby Connolly. They just barely whipped things into shape in time for the Broadway opening. To add authenticity to the show, the nominal sponsor was Ziegfeld's widow, Billie Burke, and the leading comic attraction was *Follies* veteran Fanny Brice. Miss Brice did takeoffs on evangelist Aimee Semple MacPherson and strip-tease dancers, impersonated a bratty child known as Baby Snooks, and appeared with another great clown, Willie Howard, in a frantic burlesque of the play *Sailor, Beware!* The durable "I Like the Likes of You" was sung in the show by Robert Cummings and danced to by Vilma and Buddy Ebsen.

ANYTHING GOES

Music & lyrics:
Cole Porter

Book:
**Guy Bolton & P.G. Wodehouse,
Howard Lindsay & Russel Crouse**

Producer:
Vinton Freedley

Director:
Howard Lindsay

Choreographer:
Robert Alton

Cast:
**William Gaxton, Ethel Merman,
Victor Moore, Bettina Hall,
Vera Dunn, Leslie Barrie,
Vivian Vance, Helen Raymond,
George E. Mack, Houston Richards**

Songs:
**"I Get A Kick Out Of You";
"There'll Always Be a Lady Fair";
"All Through the Night";
"You're the Top";
"Anything Goes";
"Blow, Gabriel, Blow";
"Be Like the Bluebird";
"The Gypsy in Me"**

New York run:
Alvin Theatre, November 21, 1934; 420 p.

Anything Goes. Ethel Merman leading the chorus in "Blow, Gabriel, Blow." (Vandamm)

*F*ollowing the debacle of a musical comedy called *Pardon My English* early in 1933, producer Vinton Freedley had to flee the country to avoid creditors. To help clear his mind and regain his health, Freedley spent most of his time in a fishing boat off the Pearl Islands in the Gulf of Panama. While fishing he envisaged the perfect musical comedy with which he would launch his comeback: William Gaxton, Victor Moore, and Ethel Merman would play the leading roles, the score would be written by Cole Porter, and the libretto would be by the veteran team of Guy Bolton and P.G. Wodehouse who would tie everything together in a fun-filled story about a group of oddball characters on an ocean liner that is facing a possible shipwreck.

Once he returned to New York and paid off his debts, the producer rounded up his people for what was originally called *Bon Voyage,* then *Hard to Get.* With rehearsals about to begin, disaster struck when the *S.S. Morro Castle* went down in flames off the New Jersey coast with a loss of over 125 lives. Obviously, the script had to be changed. Since Bolton and Wodehouse were then in Europe, Freedley, in desperation, turned to his director, Howard Lindsay, who agreed to undertake the rewriting with a press agent and part-time librettist named Russel Crouse (thereby launching the celebrated team that would be responsible for a total of seven musical-comedy librettos and eight plays).

Though still taking place on shipboard, the new story eliminated the shipwreck but retained the leading characters of the original plot: nightclub singer Reno Sweeney (Merman), her chum Billy Crocker (Gaxton) who stows away to be near Hope Harcourt (Bettina Hall), the debutante he loves, and Moon-Face Mooney (Moore), Public Enemy No. 13, who masquerades as a clergyman to avoid the long arm of the FBI. It may have been created out of tragedy, but *Anything Goes* (the title was chosen to indicate the desperation with which the show was put together) turned out to be the fourth longest running musical of the Thirties as well as one of the decade's most durable attractions. Porter's score, considered his best to date, included three Merman trademarks — "I Get a Kick Out of You," "You're the Top" (a duet with Gaxton), and "Blow, Gabriel, Blow." During the Broadway run, Miss Merman was succeeded by Benay Venuta.

Anything Goes was revived Off Broadway in 1962 with Hal Linden, Eileen Rodgers, and Mickey Deems, and a number of Porter interpolations. It ran 239 performances. In 1987, it was given a new production at Lincoln Center's Vivian Beaumont Theatre, which had the longest run of all. During the engagement, Patti luPone was succeeded by Leslie Uggams, Howard McGillin by Gregg Edelman. The 1936 film version offered Ethel Merman plus Bing Crosby and Charlie Ruggles; the 1956 film of the same name, also with Crosby, had nothing in common with the original except for five songs.

Porgy And Bess

Music:
George Gershwin

Lyrics:
**DuBose Heyward,
Ira Gershwin**

Book:
DuBose Heyward

Producer:
Theatre Guild

Director:
Rouben Mamoulian

Cast:
**Todd Duncan, Anne Brown,
Warren Coleman, John W. Bubbles,
Abbie Mithcell, Ruby Elzy,
Georgette Harvey, Edward Matthews,
Helen Dowdy, J. Rosamond Johnson**

Songs:
**"Summertime" (Heyward);
"A Woman Is a Sometime Thing" (Heyward);
"My Man's Gone Now" (Heyward);
"I Got Plenty o' Nuttin'" (Heyward, Gershwin);
"Bess, You Is My Woman Now" (Heyward,
Gershwin);
"It Ain't Necessarily So" (Gershwin);
"I Loves You, Porgy" (Heyward, Gershwin);
"There's a Boat Dat's Leavin' Soon
for New York" (Gershwin);
"I'm on My Way" (Heyward)**

New York run:
Alvin Theatre, October 10, 1935; 124 p.

Porgy and Bess. Ruby Elzy and J. Rosamond Johnson in the saucer burial scene. Anne Brown and Todd Duncan are to their left. (Vandamm)

*U*niversally accepted as the most popular opera written by an American composer, *Porgy and Bess* began life in 1925 as the novel *Porgy* by DuBose Heyward. Heyward's setting of Catfish Row in Charleston, South Carolina, and his dramatic story of the crippled beggar Porgy, the seductive Bess, the menacing Crown, and the slinky cocaine dealer Sportin' Life fired George Gershwin's imagination even before Heyward and his wife, Dorothy, adapted the book into a play two years later. After a number of delays, Gershwin began writing the opera late in 1933 with Heyward as librettist-lyricist and brother Ira Gershwin as co-lyricist. The composer's last Broadway score, the work was completed — including Gershwin's own orchestrations — in 20 months.

The initial production, with Todd Duncan and Anne Brown in the leads, was treated as such a major event that the larger dailies dispatched both their drama and music critics to cover the opening. It was not, however, a commercial success, though many of the solos and duets — "Summertime," "Bess, You Is My Woman Now," "I Got Plenty O' Nuttin'," "It Ain't Necessarily So" — soon caught on. Four revivals of *Porgy and Bess* have had extended Broadway runs. In

Porgy and Bess. The setting of Catfish Row, designed by Sergei Soudeikine. (Vandamm)

In 1942, again with Todd Duncan and Anne Brown but with Avon Long replacing John W. Bubbles as Sportin' Life, the musical ran successfully for 286 performances (at a $2.75 top ticket price) in a somewhat streamlined version with a smaller orchestra and no recitative. It was produced by Cheryl Crawford and directed by Robert Ross. The production then toured for 17 months, including a two-month return visit to New York. Ten years later, one of the most ambitious projects in theatre history was inaugurated with a four-year international tour directed by co-producer Robert Breen. Still more musical drama than opera, *Porgy and Bess* was performed in 23 cities in the United States and Canada, and — under the auspices of the State Department — in 28 countries throughout Europe (including well-publicized engagements in Leningrad and Moscow), the Middle East and Latin America. This company's 1953 stay in New York had the longest run the work has had to date.

A mounting in 1976 by the Houston Grand Opera was staged at the Uris (now the Gershwin) Theatre on 51st Street west of Broadway. With an acclaimed performance by Clamma Dale as Bess and all the original musical portions restored, the production came closest to the composer's concept of the work as an opera. It was also the basis for the 1983 revival, the first adult, full-scale dramatic work ever staged at the 6,000-seat Radio City Music Hall. Two years later, on its 50th anniversary, *Porgy and Bess* entered the repertory of the Metropolitan Opera. In 1959, a screen adaptation was released with Sidney Poitier, Dorothy Dandridge, and Sammy Davis Jr.

JUMBO

Music:
Richard Rodgers

Lyrics:
Lorenz Hart

Book:
Ben Hecht & Charles MacArthur

Producer:
Bill Rose

Directors:
John Murray Anderson, George Abbott

Choreographer:
Allan K. Foster

Cast:
Jimmy Durante, Paul Whiteman Orchestra, Donald Novis, Gloria Grafton, A. P. Kaye, A. Robins, Poodles Hanneford, Big Rosie, Tilda Getze

Songs:
**"Over and Over Again";
"The Circus Is on Parade";
"The Most Beautiful Girl in the World";
"My Romance";
"Little Girl Blue"**

New York run:
Hippodrome, November 16, 1935; 233 p.

*T*he Hippodrome, once located on 43rd Street and 6th Avenue, was a huge barn of a theatre that had not been in use for five years when showman Billy Rose decided that it would be just the place to house the spectacular circus musical he named *Jumbo*. Designer Albert Johnson completely rebuilt the auditorium to make it resemble an actual circus, with a grandstand sloping up from a single circular revolving stage. The show marked the first of 34 musicals directed by George Abbott as well as the return to Broadway of Rodgers and Hart after almost three years in Hollywood. Plotted by Ben Hecht and Charles MacArthur to give plenty of opportunity for the specialty acts recruited from all over the world, the book had to do with a debt-ridden circus and what the well-meaning but inept publicity man Claudius B. Bowers (Jimmy Durante) does to help save the day. *Jumbo* cost an unprecedented $340,000 to open; it closed after rehearsing for six months and playing for five. The evening's highlight: the blue-tinted first-act finale, "Little Girl Blue," in which heroine Gloria Grafton (who had replaced Ella Logan before the premiere) dreams she is a child again being entertained by her favorite circus performers. Durante was also in the 1962 screen version, along with Doris Day and Martha Raye.

JUBILEE

Music & lyrics:
Cole Porter

Book:
Moss Hart

Producers:
Sam H. Harris & Max Gordon

Directors:
Hassard Short, Monty Woolley

Choreographer:
Albertina Rasch

Cast:
**Mary Boland, June Knight,
Melville Cooper, Charles Walters,
Derek Williams, Mark Plant,
Montgomery Clift, May Boley,
Margaret Adams**

Songs:
**"Why Shouldn't I?";
"Begin the Beguine";
"A Picture of Me Without You";
"Me and Marie";
"Just One of Those Things"**

New York run:
**Imperial Theatre,
October 12, 1935; 169 p.**

Jubilee. Mary Boland and Melville Cooper singing "Me and Marie." (Vandamm)

*S*eeking suitable inspiration for an elegant song-and-dance entertainment, Cole Porter and Moss Hart took off on a four-and-a-half month, 34,000-mile cruise around the world. Their hegira resulted in an airy concoction sparked by the recent Silver Jubilee of Britain s King George V and Queen Mary. The tale concerns itself with what might happen if members of a mythical royal family — thanks to a supposed uprising — were given the chance to do what they wanted while gadding about town incognito. King Melville Cooper spends his time perfecting sleight-of-hand tricks, Queen Mary Boland is thrilled to meet Mowgli the movie ape man, Prince Charles Walters learns how to begin the beguine from dancer June Knight, and Princess Margaret Adams answers her own question in "Why Shouldn't I?" by having just one of those crazy flings with a Noel Coward-type playwright. Then it's back to the pomp and circumstance of the royal jubilee. Though beloved by her theatre-going subjects, Miss Boland had to return to Hollywood after only four months; her successor Laura Hope Crews couldn't keep the celebration going a month.

ON YOUR TOES

Music:
Richard Rodgers

Lyrics:
Lorenz Hart

Book:
Richard Rodgers, Lorenz Hart & George Abbott

Producer:
Dwight Deere Wiman

Director:
**Worthington Miner
(George Abbott uncredited)**

Cast:
**Ray Bolger, Luella Gear, Tamara Geva,
Monty Woolley, Doris Carson, David Morris,
Demetrios Vilan, George Church**

Songs:
"The Three B's";
"It's Got to Be Love";
"Too Good for the Average Man";
"There's a Small Hotel";
"The Heart Is Quicker Than the Eye";
"Quiet Night";
"Glad to Be Unhappy";
"On Your Toes";
"Slaughter on Tenth Avenue" (ballet)

New York run:
Imperial Theatre, April 11, 1936; 315 p.

On Your Toes. Luella Gear, Monty Woolley, Ray Bolger, and Demetrios Vilan.

*O**n Your Toes** made a star of rubberlegged dancer Ray Bolger, and it also gave George Balanchine his first opportunity to create dances for a book musical. Most important, it signaled a major breakthrough in form by utilizing ballet as an integral part of the story. Junior Dolan (Bolger), an ex-vaudevillian now teaching music at Knickerbocker University, a WPA extension in New York, enlists the help of patroness Peggy Porterfield (Luella Gear) to persuade Sergei Alexandrovich (Monty Woolley), the director of the Russian Ballet, to stage a friend's jazzy "Slaughter on Tenth Avenue" ballet. While he may dream of sharing the pleasures of a small hotel with girlfriend Frankie Frayne (Doris Carson), Junior becomes involved with the company's prima ballerina, Vera Barnova (Tamara Geva), and even takes over the male lead in "Slaughter." This so enrages Vera's lover and regular dancing partner that he hires two thugs to kill Junior while he is performing on stage. To avoid being a target Junior keeps dancing even after the ballet is over, then — once the gunmen have been arrested — falls exhausted to the floor.

On Your Toes. Ray Bolger, George Church, and Tamara Geva in a dramatic moment from "Slaughter on Tenth Avenue." (White)

Richard Rodgers and Lorenz Hart had originally written the musical as a movie vehicle for Fred Astaire, but the dancer turned it down because he was afraid his public would not accept him without his trademark attire of top hat, white tie and tails. The team then rewrote the script as a stage musical and Lee Shubert took an option on it with Ray Bolger set for the male lead. When Shubert lost interest, the rights were picked up by Dwight Deere Wiman (it was the first of five Rodgers and Hart shows he would produce), with George Abbott joining the project as co-author and director. Production delays, however, prompted Abbott to withdraw as director, though he did return to restage the musical after its poorly-received Boston opening. Originally, Marilyn Miller and Gregory Ratoff were sought for the roles that went to Miss Geva and Mr. Woolley.

There have been two revivals of *On Your Toes* on Broadway. In 1954, Abbott and Balanchine put together a production starring Bobby Van, Vera Zorina (she had appeared in the role of the ballerina in London and in the movie version), and Elaine Stritch (who played Peggy and sang the interpolated "You Took Advantage of Me"). The general verdict was that the musical was hopelessly dated and it remained only two months. Twenty-nine years later, however, again staged by Abbott, it succeeded so well that it bested the original Broadway run. Natalia Makarova of the American Ballet Theatre made an impressive Main Stem debut in the show. She was replaced during the engagement by ballerinas Galina Panova and Valentina Kozlova, and Dina Merrill was replaced by Kitty Carlisle. The 1939 movie, with Eddie Albert as Junior, used music only as background and for the ballets.

ZIEGFELD FOLLIES

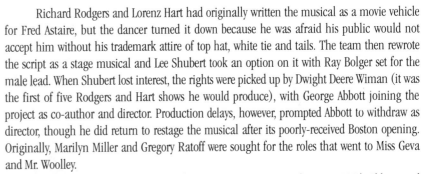

Music: **Vernon Duke**

Lyrics: **Ira Gershwin**

Sketches: **David Freedman**

Producer: **Billie Burke Ziegfeld
(Messrs. Shubert uncredited)**

Directors: **John Murray Anderson,
Edward Clark Lilley**

Choreographers:
Robert Alton, George Balanchine

Cast:
**Fanny Brice, Bob Hope, Gertrude Niesen,
Josephine Baker, Hugh O'Connell,
Harriet Hoctor, Eve Arden, Judy Canova,
Cherry & June Preisser, Nicholas Brothers,
John Hoysradt, Stan Kavanaugh**

Songs:
**"Island in the West Indies"; "Words Without
Music"; "That Moment of Moments";
"I Can't Get Started"**

New York run:
Winter Garden, January 30, 1936; 115 p.

*F*anny Brice returned for her second Shubert-sponsored *Ziegfeld Follies* (it was her 15th and final Broadway show), along with a number of holdovers from the 1934 edition. They were joined by ballet choreographer George Balanchine making his Broadway debut. The revue was deemed superior to its predecessor, with Miss Brice up to her old shtick kidding modern dancing and playing Baby Snooks, and Bob Hope getting the chance to butter up Eve Arden in the classic "I Can't Get Started." Another highlight was the first-act finale spoofing the latest Hollywood extravaganza, "The Broadway Gold Melody Diggers of 42nd Street." The *Follies* reopened in the fall for 112 additional performances with Jane Pickens, Gypsy Rose Lee, and Cass Daley joining the cast.

RED, HOT AND BLUE!

Music & lyrics:
Cole Porter

Book:
Howard Lindsay & Russel Crouse

Producer:
Vinton Freedley

Director:
Howard Lindsay

Choreographer:
George Hale

Cast:
Jimmy Durante, Ethel Merman,
Bob Hope, Polly Walters,
Paul & Grace Hartman,
Vivian Vance, Lew Parker

Songs:
"Ours";
"Down in the Depths (on the Ninetieth Floor)";
"You've Got Something";
"It's De-Lovely";
"Ridin' High";
"Red, Hot and Blue"

New York run:
Alvin Theatre, October 29, 1936; 183 p.

Red, Hot and Blue! Ethel Merman and Bob Hope. (Vandamm)

*A*nxious to repeat the success of *Anything Goes,* producer Vinton Freedley signed its three stars and its three writers for his next musical, *Red, Hot and Blue!* But after overhearing Freedley promise Ethel Merman that hers would be the most prominent role, William Gaxton and Victor Moore bowed out and were replaced by Bob Hope and Jimmy Durante. The show, which seemed to be aiming for *Of Thee I Sing*-type political satire, offered Miss Merman as Nails O'Reilly Duquesne, a manicurist-turned-wealthy widow, Hope as Bob Hale, her lawyer and love interest, and Durante as Policy Pinkle, the captain of the polo team at Larks Nest Prison. Pinkle is released to help win a Congressional committee's approval for Nails and Bob's national lottery in which the first prize goes to the ticket holder who finds a girl who had sat on a hot waffle iron when she was four. The Supreme Court, however, declares the lottery unconstitutional on the grounds that it might benefit the American people. Though no red hot smash, the musical served to introduce three certifiable Cole Porter standards: "It's De-Lovely," "Down in the Depths," and "Ridin' High." It is also remembered for the battle of the billing, which was resolved by crossing the names of Jimmy Durante and Ethel Merman above the show's title.

THE SHOW IS ON

Music & lyrics:
Miscellaneous writers

Sketches:
David Freedman, Moss Hart

Producers:
Messrs. Shubert

Directors:
Vincente Minnelli, Edward Clark Lilley

Choreographer:
Robert Alton, Harry Losee

Cast:
**Beatrice Lillie, Bert Lahr,
Reginald Gardiner, Mitzi Mayfair,
Paul Haakon, Gracie Barrie,
Charles Walters, Vera Allen, Jack McCauley**

Songs:
**"Now" (Vernon Duke-Ted Fetter); "Rhythm"
(Richard Rodgers-Lorenz Hart); "Song of the
Woodman" (Harold Arlen-E.Y. Harburg);
"Long as You've Got Your Health" (Will Irwin-
Harburg, Norman Zeno); "By Strauss" (George
Gershwin-Ira Gershwin); "Little Old Lady"
(Hoagy Carmichael-Stanley Adams)**

New York run:
Winter Garden, December 25, 1936; 237 p.

Note that Vincente Minnelli's name is misspelled twice.

*T*he fifth and final mid-Thirties revue presented by the Shuberts at the Winter Garden was one of the brightest, merriest, and most elegant of the decade's stage attractions. Featuring two superior clowns, Beatrice Lillie and Bert Lahr, *The Show Is On* was something of a successor to *At Home Abroad,* only this time the theme was around the world of show business. In songs, sketches, and production numbers, it looked in on a variety of phenomena and events — from excessively rhythmic pop singers to raffish burlesque shows, from John Gielgud's production of *Hamlet* (which is ruined by the outbursts of Miss Lillie's boorish socialite) to coquettish music-hall entertainers (Miss Lillie perched on a migratory half moon dispensing garters to favored gentlemen), and from he-man concert baritones (Lahr's classic "Song of the Woodman") to an old-fashioned tent show production of *Uncle Tom's Cabin. The Show Is On* returned briefly in the fall of 1937 with Rose King and Willie Howard.

BABES IN ARMS

Music:
Richard Rodgers

Lyrics:
Lorenz Hart

Book:
Richard Rodgers & Lorenz Hart

Producer:
Dwight Deere Wiman

Director:
Robert Sinclair

Choreographer:
George Balanchine

Cast:
**Mitzi Green, Wynn Murray, Ray Heatherton,
Duke McHale, Alfred Drake,
Ray McDonald, Grace McDonald,
Nicholas Brothers, Dan Dailey**

Songs:
**"Where or When";
"Babes in Arms";
"I Wish I Were in Love Again";
"My Funny Valentine";
"Johnny One Note";
"Imagine";
"All at Once" ;
"The Lady Is a Tramp";
"You Are So Fair"**

New York run:
Shubert Theatre, April 14, 1937; 289 p.

With such songs as "I Wish I Were in Love Again," "Johnny One Note," "The Lady Is a Tramp," "My Funny Valentine," and "Where or When," *Babes in Arms* could claim more hits than any other Rodgers and Hart musical. In the high-spirited, youthful show, a group of teenagers, whose parents are out-of-work vaudevillians, stage a revue to keep from being sent to a work farm. Unfortunately, the show is a bomb. Later, when a transatlantic French flyer lands nearby, they are able to attract enough publicity to put on a successful show and build their own youth center. Because the sets were modest and the cast boasted no stellar names, producer Dwight Deere Wiman priced his tickets at a $3.85 top. Among the show's Broadway debuts were those of Alfred Drake (he sang the title song) and Dan Dailey. The 1939 movie version featured Judy Garland and Mickey Rooney.

I'D RATHER BE RIGHT

Music:
Richard Rodgers

Lyrics:
Lorenz Hart

Book:
George S. Kaufman & Moss Hart

Producer:
Sam H. Harris

Director:
George S. Kaufman

Choreographers:
Charles Weidman, Ned McGurn

Cast:
George M. Cohan, Taylor Holmes,
Joy Hodges, Austin Marshall,
Marion Green, Mary Jane Walsh

Songs:
"Have You Met Miss Jones?";
"Sweet Sixty-Five";
"We're Going to Balance the Budget";
"I'd Rather Be Right";
"Off the Record"

New York run:
Alvin Theatre, November 2, 1937; 290 p.

I'd Rather Be Right. George M. Cohan as President Franklin D. Roosevelt giving a 4th of July speech. (Vandamm)

I'd Rather Be Right was the most anxiously awaited theatrical event of the decade for two reasons: the central character was President Franklin D. Roosevelt and the part was being played by the legendary George M. Cohan, who was returning to the musical stage for the first time in ten years in the only song-and-dance show he ever appeared in that he did not write himself. The work, however, was considered not quite up to the satirical standards set by *Of Thee I Sing,* with which it was most frequently compared. The locale is New York's Central Park on the 4th of July. Peggy and Phil (Joy Hodges and Austin Marshall) hope to get married but Phil's boss won't give him a raise until Roosevelt balances the budget. Phil falls asleep and dreams that they meet FDR strolling through the park. After Phil explains the couple's dilemma, Roosevelt promises to help — which is only an excuse for some genial ribbing at the expense of Cabinet members, the Supreme Court, the PWA, fireside chats, Alf Landon, press conferences, and the President s decision to seek a third term.

THE BOYS FROM SYRACUSE

Music:
Richard Rodgers

Lyrics:
Lorenz Hart

Book:
George Abbott

Producer-director:
George Abbott

Choreographer:
George Balanchine

Cast:
Jimmy Savo, Teddy Hart, Eddie Albert,
Wynn Murray, Ronald Graham,
Muriel Angelus, Marcy Wescott,
Betty Bruce, Burl Ives

Songs:
"Falling in Love With Love";
"The Shortest Day of the Year";
"This Can't Be Love";
"He and She";
"You Have Cast Your Shadow on the Sea";
"Sing for Your Supper";
"What Can You Do With a Man?"

New York run:
Alvin Theatre, November 23, 1938; 235 p.

The Boys from Syracuse. Marcy Wescott, Wynn Murray, and Muriel Angelus singing "Sing for Your Supper." (Vandamm)

*T*he genesis of *The Boys from Syracuse* began when Rodgers and Hart, while working on another show, were discussing the fact that no one had yet written a Broadway musical based on a play by Shakespeare. Their obvious choice was *The Comedy of Errors* (whose plot Shakespeare had borrowed from Plautus' *Menaechmi),* partly because Hart's brother, Teddy Hart, was always being confused with another comic actor, Jimmy Savo. The action takes place in Ephesus in ancient Asia Minor, and the mildly ribald tale concerns the efforts of two boys from Syracuse, Antipholus and his servant Dromio (Eddie Albert and Jimmy Savo), to find their long-lost twins who — for reasons of plot confusion — are also named Antipholus and Dromio (Ronald Graham and Teddy Hart). Complications arise when the wives of the Ephesians, Adriana (Muriel Angelus) and her servant Luce (Wynn Murray), mistake the two strangers for their husbands, though the couples eventually get sorted out after Adriana's sister

The Boys from Syracuse. Betty Bruce, Teddy Hart, and Eddie Albert. (Vandamm)

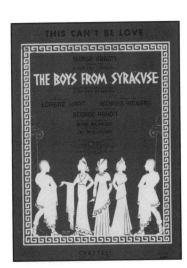

Luciana (Marcy Wescott) and the Syracuse Antipholus admit their love while protesting "This Can't Be Love." In 1963, an Off-Broadway revival had a longer run than the original. Allan Jones, Joe Penner, and Martha Raye were in the 1940 film. In 1981, *Oh, Brother!,* a second musical adaptation of the same basic tale had a brief stay on Broadway. Other musicals inspired by Shakespeare have been *Swingin' the Dream* (1939) and *Babes in the Wood* (1964), both from *A Midsummer Night's Dream; Kiss Me, Kate* (1948), from *The Taming of the Shrew; West Side Story* (1957) and *Sensations* (1970), both from *Romeo and Juliet; Love and Let Love* (1968), *Your Own Thing* (1968), and *Music Is* (1976), all from *Twelfth Night; Two Gentlemen of Verona* (1971); and *Rockabye Hamlet* (1976).

LEAVE IT TO ME

Music & lyrics:
Cole Porter

Book:
Bella & Samuel Spewack

Producer:
Vinton Freedley

Director:
Samuel Spewack

Choreographer:
Robert Alton

Cast:
**William Gaxton, Victor Moore,
Sophie Tucker, Tamara, Mary Martin,
Edward H. Robins, Alexander Asro,
George Tobias, Gene Kelly**

Songs:
**"Get Out of Town";
"From Now On";
"Most Gentlemen Don't Like Love";
"My Heart Belongs to Daddy";
"I Want to Go Home"**

New York run:
Imperial Theatre, November 9, 1938; 291 p.

Leave It to Me! Mary Martin. (Vandamm)

With a book distantly related to their own play, *Clear All Wires,* Bella and Samuel Spewack came up with a spoof of Communism and U.S. diplomacy that offered comedian Victor Moore one of his meatiest roles as mild-mannered Alonzo P. "Stinky" Goodhue. Goodhue is unwillingly named Ambassador to the Soviet Union because his ambitious wife (Sophie Tucker) has contributed generously to President Roosevelt's re-election campaign. Aided by foreign correspondent Buckley Joyce Thomas (William Gaxton), the Ambassador does everything he can to be recalled, but each blunder only succeeds in making him a bigger hero. Finally, he introduces a plan to ensure world peace — which, of course, no one wants — and Stinky is soon happily on his way back to Kansas. Mary Martin made a notable Broadway debut in *Leave It to Me!,* singing and coyly stripping to "My Heart Belongs to Daddy" while being stranded on a Siberian railroad station with a male quartet that included Gene Kelly. Two months after the musical closed it paid a two-week return visit to New York.

KNICKERBOCKER HOLIDAY

Music:
Kurt Weill

Lyrics & book:
Maxwell Anderson

Producer:
Playwrights' Company

Director:
Joshua Logan

Choreographers:
Carl Randall, Edwin Denby

Cast:
**Walter Huston, Ray Middleton,
Jeanne Madden, Richard Kollmar,
Robert Rounseville, Howard Freeman,
Clarence Nordstrom**

Songs:
**"There's Nowhere to Go but Up";
"It Never Was You";
"How Can You Tell an American?";
"September Song";
"The Scars"**

New York run:
**Ethel Barrymore Theatre,
October 19, 1938; 168 p.**

Knickerbocker Holiday. Walter Huston, Jeanne Madden, and ladies of New Amsterdam. (Lucas)

A victim of Hitler's Germany, Kurt Weill settled in New York to become one of the Broadway theatre's most admired and influential composers. For *Knickerbocker Holiday,* the second of his eight American works, he was joined by playwright Maxwell Anderson to create what was probably the first musical to use an historical subject as the means through which views on contemporary matters could be expressed. Here the theme was totalitarianism versus democracy, as personified by Pieter Stuyvesant (Walter Huston), the autocratic governor of New Amsterdam in 1647, and Brom Broeck (Richard Kollmar), the freedom-loving "first American" who is opposed to any kind of government interference. The point became somewhat muddied when it appeared that Anderson's target was President Roosevelt rather than any of the peace-menacing dictators then in power. There was confusion of a more dramatic kind since Walter Huston, in his only Broadway musical, made Stuyvesant such a likable chap — especially when he sang of the anxieties of growing old in "September Song" — that audience sympathies tended to be with the wrong man. The 1944 screen version featured Nelson Eddy and Charles Coburn.

TOO MANY GIRLS

Music:
Richard Rodgers

Lyrics:
Lorenz Hart

Book:
George Marion Jr.

Producer-director:
George Abbott

Choreographer:
Robert Alton

Cast:
Marcy Wescott, Desi Arnez, Hal LeRoy,
Mary Jane Walsh, Diosa Costello,
Richard Kollmar, Eddie Bracken,
Leila Ernst, Van Johnson

Songs:
"Love Never Went to College";
"Spic and Spanish";
"I Like to Recognize the Tune";
"I Didn't Know What Time It Was";
"She Could Shake the Maracas";
"Give It Back to the Indians"

New York run:
Imperial Theatre, October 18, 1939; 249 p.

Too Many Girls. Eddie Bracken and Hal LeRoy help an inebriated Desi Arnez confront Marcy Wescott. (Vandamm)

*B*y 1939 — after such shows as *Leave It to Jane* and *Good News!* — a rah-rah college musical about football may not have been the most original idea along the Main Stem, but blessed with spirited songs by Rodgers and Hart, a youthful, talented cast, and fast-paced direction by George Abbott, *Too Many Girls* won high marks with both critics and public. Set in Pottawatomie College, Stop Gap, New Mexico (described as "one of those colleges that play football on Friday"), the musical featured an All-American backfield composed of Desi Arnaz, Hal LeRoy, Richard Kollmar (succeeded by Van Johnson for the tour), and Eddie Bracken, who also, unknown to her, act as bodyguards for wealthy coed Marcy Wescott. Soon boy students are pairing off with girl students, and Kollmar and Wescon get the chance to voice such sentiments as "Love Never Went to College" and "I Didn't Know What Time It Was." The 1940 movie version with Lucille Ball and Ann Miller also included members of the original cast.

DUBARRY WAS A LADY

Music & lyrics:
Cole Porter

Book:
Herbert Fields & B. G. DeSylva

Producer:
B. G. DeSylva

Choreographer:
Robert Alton

Cast:
Bert Lahr, Ethel Merman, Betty Grable,
Benny Baker, Ronald Graham,
Charles Walters, Kay Sutton

Songs:
"When Love Beckoned (in Fifty-Second Street)";
"Well, Did You Evah?";
"But in the Morning, No";
"Do I Love You?";
"It Was Written in the Stars";
"Give Him the Oo-la-la";
"Katie Went to Haiti";
"Friendship"

New York run:
46th Street Theatre, December 6, 1939; 408 p.

DuBarry Was a Lady. Bert Lahr and Ethel Merman.

*B*roadway's fifth longest-running musical of the Thirties, *DuBarry Was a Lady* was the first of three smash hits offered in succession by producer B.G. DeSylva. The show evolved through the merging of two ideas: Herbert Fields wanted to write a musical with Mae West as DuBarry and DeSylva wanted to write one about a washroom attendant in a swanky New York nightclub who is smitten by a Brenda Frazier-type debutante. Both concepts were combined by having the attendant, named Louis Blore, switch his affections to May Daly, the club's flashy singing star, and by having Louis — after taking a mickey finn — dream that he is King Louis XV and the singer his unaccommodating concubine. Ethel Merman and Bert Lahr, who stopped the show nightly with their raucous avowal of eternal friendship, were hailed as Broadway's royal couple, and Betty Grable won such favorable notice that she was soon whisked off to Hollywood stardom. During the Broadway run, Miss Merman was succeeded by Gypsy Rose Lee and Frances Williams. The show's movie version, in 1943, featured Lucille Ball, Gene Kelly, and Red Skelton.

STRIKE UP THE BAND

(From "STRIKE UP THE BAND")

Words by IRA GERSHWIN
Music by GEORGE GERSHWIN

Lyrics in the score:

There is work to be done, to be done! There's a war to be won, to be won! Come, you
Yan-kee Doo, Doo-dle-oo, Doo-dle-oo, We'll come through, Doo-dle-oo, Doo-dle-oo, For the

son of a son of a gun! Take your stand! _____ Fall in line, yea bo! _____
red, white and blue, Doo-dle-oo, Lend a hand! _____ With our flag un-furled, _____

Come a-long, let's go! _____ Hey, lead-er! Strike up the
For a brave new world! _____ Hey, lead-er! Strike up the

band! _____ Let the band! _____

FINE AND DANDY

(From "FINE AND DANDY")

Lyric by PAUL JAMES
Music by KAY SWIFT

EMBRACEABLE YOU

Words by IRA GERSHWIN
Music by GEORGE GERSHWIN

I GOT RHYTHM
(From "GIRL CRAZY")

Words by IRA GERSHWIN
Music by GEORGE GERSHWIN

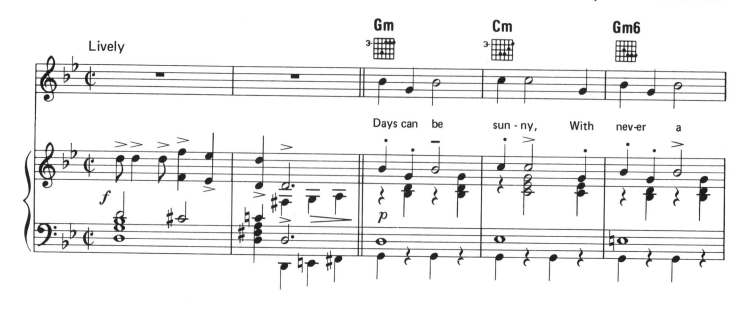

Days can be sun-ny, With nev-er a sigh;

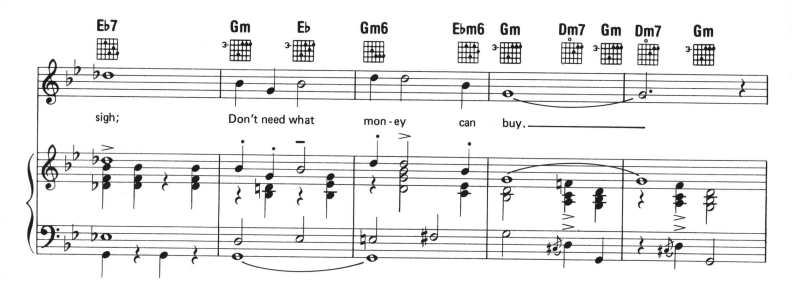

Don't need what mon-ey can buy.

Birds in the tree sing their day-ful of song, Why should-n't

BUT NOT FOR ME

Words by IRA GERSHWIN
Music by GEORGE GERSHWIN

LOVE FOR SALE

Words and Music by COLE PORTER

Smooth "Country" beat

BODY AND SOUL

Words by EDWARD HEYMAN,
ROBERT SOUR and FRANK EYTON
Music by JOHN GREEN

Moderately, smoothly

DANCING IN THE DARK
(From "THE BAND WAGON")

Words by HOWARD DIETZ
Music by ARTHUR SCHWARTZ

Slowly with expression

Danc - ing in the dark _____ Till the tune ends, We're danc - ing in the dark _____ And it soon ends; We're waltz - ing in the

Life Is Just A Bowl Of Cherries

Words and Music by LEW BROWN
and RAY HENDERSON

OF THEE I SING

Words by
IRA GERSHWIN

Music by
GEORGE GERSHWIN

THE NIGHT
WAS MADE FOR LOVE

Words by OTTO HARBACH
Music by JEROME KERN

Let's Have Another Cup O' Coffee

*) Tune Ukulele
or Banjulele Banjo

G C E A

By
IRVING BERLIN

*) Letters over diagrams are names of
the chords in original key and are
adaptable to Banjo or Guitar.

Why wor-ry when skies are gray

Why should we com - plain

Let's laugh at the cloud-y day

just an A - pril show'r, E - ven John D. Rock - e - fel - ler is

look - ing for the sil - ver lin - ing. Mis - ter Her - bert Hoov - er says that

now's the time to buy, So let's have an - oth - er cup o' - cof - fee And

let's have an - oth - er piece o' - pie! pie!

"SOFT LIGHTS AND SWEET MUSIC"

*) Tune Ukulele
or Banjulele Banjo

G C E A

By IRVING BERLIN

*) Letters over diagrams are names of
the chords in original key and are
adaptable to Banjo or Guitar

I can't re - sist the moan of a cel - lo,

I can't re - sist the light of the moon,

CHORUS

Soft lights _____ and sweet mu - sic, And you in _____ my arms, _____

Soft lights and sweet mel - o - dy, _____ Will bring you clo - ser to me; _____ Cho - pin _____ and

THE SONG IS YOU

Lyrics by **OSCAR HAMMERSTEIN** II / Music by **JEROME KERN**

MUSIC IN THE AIR (1932)

I've Told Ev'ry Little Star

Words by OSCAR HAMMERSTEIN II
Music by JEROME KERN

YOU'RE AN OLD SMOOTHIE

Words by
B.G. DeSYLVA

Music by
RICHARD A. WHITING and HERB BROWN NACIO

Moderato

You're the smooth-est so and so,— Not on-ly that, you're might-y— cute; You're

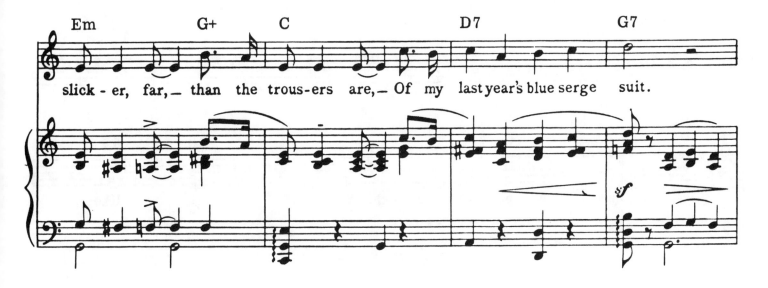

slick-er, far,— than the trous-ers are,— Of my last year's blue serge suit.

NIGHT AND DAY
(From "THE GAY DIVORCE")

Words and Music by
COLE PORTER

A SHINE ON YOUR SHOES

Words and Music by
HOWARD DIETZ and
ARTHUR SCHWARTZ

Don't you be a good for noth-in', Nev-er 'mount to noth-in', Hang-in' round the cor-ners!

Can't you see you nev-er will be get-tin' an-y-where.

HEAT WAVE

By
IRVING BERLIN

*) Symbols for Guitar, Chords for Ukulele and Banjo.

The CAN-CAN is real-ly the rea - son __ why. ____

CHORUS

We're hav-ing a HEAT WAVE ____ A trop-i-cal HEAT WAVE ____

____ The temp'-ra-ture's ris - ing, __ It is - n't sur-pris - ing, __ She

cer-tain-ly can __ CAN - CAN She start-ed the HEAT WAVE ____

D. S. al Fine

Yesterdays

Words by OTTO HARBACH
Music by JEROME KERN

Smoke Gets In Your Eyes

Words by OTTO HARBACH
Music by JEROME KERN

WAGON WHEELS

Words by BILLY HILL
Music by PETER DeROSE

I GET A KICK OUT OF YOU

"Anything Goes"

Words and Music by
COLE PORTER

Moderato

VERSE

My sto-ry is

much too sad to be told, But prac-tic-'ly ev-'ry-thing leaves me to-tal-ly

cold. The on-ly ex-cep-tion I know is the case

When I'm out on a qui-et spree Fight-ing vain-ly the old en-nui,

ANYTHING GOES

Words and Music by
COLE PORTER

SUMMERTIME

(From "PORGY AND BESS")

Words by DuBOSE HEYWARD
Music by GEORGE GERSHWIN

116

I Got Plenty O' Nuttin'

Words by Ira Gershwin and Dubose Heyward
Music by George Gershwin

Moderately Fast

It Ain't Necessarily So

Words by IRA GERSHWIN
Music by GEORGE GERSHWIN

JUST ONE OF THOSE THINGS

Words and Music by
COLE PORTER

Rhythmically

It was Just One Of Those Things,_____

Just one____ of those cra - zy flings.____ One of those

bells that now and then rings, Just One____ Of Those

BEGIN THE BEGUINE
(From "JUBILEE")

Words & Music by COLE PORTER

MY ROMANCE
(From "JUMBO")

Words by LORENZ HART
Music by RICHARD RODGERS

LITTLE GIRL BLUE

(From "JUMBO")

Words by LORENZ HART
Music by RICHARD RODGERS

I CAN'T GET STARTED

(From "ZIEGFELD FOLLIES — 1936")

Words by IRA GERSHWIN
Music by VERNON DUKE

THERE'S A SMALL HOTEL
(From "ON YOUR TOES")

Words by LORENZ HART
Music by RICHARD RODGERS

ON YOUR TOES

Lyrics by LORENZ HART

Music by RICHARD RODGERS

Chel-sea or _____ in Sut-ton Place. _____ You've got to reach the heights to win_ the race. _____

Refrain (gracefully)

See the pret-ty ap-ple top of the tree! The high-er up, the sweet-er it grows. Pick-ing fruit you've got to be_ up on your

IT'S DE-LOVELY

(From "RED, HOT AND BLUE!")

Words and Music by COLE PORTER

*Pronounced "delukes"

Ridin' High

Words and Music by COLE PORTER

BY STRAUSS
(From "THE SHOW IS ON")

Words by IRA GERSHWIN
Music by GEORGE GERSHWIN

THE LADY IS A TRAMP
(From "BABES IN ARMS")

Words by LORENZ HART
Music by RICHARD RODGERS

MY FUNNY VALENTINE
(From "BABES IN ARMS")

Words by LORENZ HART
Music by RICHARD RODGERS

WHERE OR WHEN
(From "BABES IN ARMS")

Words by LORENZ HART
Music by RICHARD RODGERS

HAVE YOU MET MISS JONES?

Lyrics by *LORENZ HART*

Music by *RICHARD RODGERS*

It hap-pened,_ I felt it hap-pen.__ I was a-wake,___ I was-n't

blind._ I did-n't think,___ I felt it hap-pen__ Now I be-

SEPTEMBER SONG
(From the Musical Play "KNICKERBOCKER HOLIDAY")

Words by MAXWELL ANDERSON
Music by KURT WEILL

When I was a young man court-ing the girls, I played me a wait - ing
game;
meet with the young men ear - ly in spring, They court you in song and
rhyme,

If a maid re - fused me with toss - ing curls, I
They woo you with words and a clo - ver ring, But

let the old earth take a coup-le of whirls, While I plied her with tears in
if you ex - am - ine the goods they bring, They have lit - tle to of - fer but the

MY HEART BELONGS TO DADDY

(From "LEAVE IT TO ME")

Words and Music by
COLE PORTER

FALLING IN LOVE WITH LOVE

Words by LORENZ HART
Music by RICHARD RODGERS

THIS CAN'T BE LOVE
(From "THE BOYS FROM SYRACUSE")

Words by LORENZ HART
Music by RICHARD RODGERS

I Didn't Know What Time It Was

Words by LORENZ HART
Music by RICHARD RODGERS

FRIENDSHIP

COLE PORTER

WELL, DID YOU EVAH?

COLE PORTER

BROADWAY MUSICALS
Show by Show

BROADWAY MUSICALS SHOW BY SHOW 1891 - 1916
33 CLASSICS FROM SHOWS SUCH AS: *ROBIN HOOD, FLORODORA, BABES IN TOYLAND, THE MERRY WIDOW,* AND MORE. SONGS INCLUDE: AFTER THE BALL • THE BOWERY • GIVE MY REGARDS TO BROADWAY • I LOVE YOU SO! (THE MERRY WIDOW WALTZ) • THE ISLE OF OUR DREAMS • KISS ME AGAIN • MARCH OF THE TOYS • MARY'S A GRAND OLD NAME • MY HERO • SIMPLE MELODY • STREETS OF NEW YORK • TOYLAND • AND MORE.
00311514 $12.95

BROADWAY MUSICALS SHOW BY SHOW 1917 - 1929
OVER 40 SONGS FROM THE ERA'S MOST POPULAR SHOWS, INCLUDING: *ZIEGFELD FOLLIES, THE STUDENT PRINCE IN HEIDELBERG, NO NO NANETTE, OH, KAY!, SHOW BOAT, FIFTY MILLION FRENCHMEN,* AND MORE. SONGS INCLUDE: THE BIRTH OF THE BLUES • CAN'T HELP LOVIN' DAT MAN • FASCINATING RHYTHM • HOW LONG HAS THIS BEEN GOING ON? • I'M JUST WILD ABOUT HARRY • OL' MAN RIVER • A PRETTY GIRL IS LIKE A MELODY • ST. LOUIS BLUES • SECOND HAND ROSE • TEA FOR TWO • YOU DO SOMETHING TO ME • YOU'RE THE CREAM IN MY COFFEE • AND MORE.
00311515 $14.95

BROADWAY MUSICALS SHOW BY SHOW 1930 - 1939
A COLLECTION OF OVER 45 SONGS FROM THE DECADE'S BIGGEST BROADWAY HITS, INCLUDING: *ANYTHING GOES, PORGY AND BESS, BABES IN ARMS, ON YOUR TOES* AND MORE. SONGS INCLUDE: BEGIN THE BEGUINE • EMBRACEABLE YOU • FALLING IN LOVE WITH LOVE • FRIENDSHIP • I GET A KICK OUT OF YOU • I GOT RHYTHM • THE LADY IS A TRAMP • MY FUNNY VALENTINE • MY HEART BELONGS TO DADDY • ON YOUR TOES • SMOKE GETS IN YOUR EYES • STRIKE UP THE BAND • SUMMERTIME • IT AIN'T NECESSARILY SO • AND MORE.
00311516 $14.95

THIS UNIQUE SERIES EXPLORES BROADWAY'S BIGGEST HITS YEAR BY YEAR AND SHOW BY SHOW. INTERESTING FACTS AND TRIVIA AS WELL AS ARRANGEMENTS FOR THE BEST SONGS FROM EACH SHOW ARE PRESENTED IN A PACKAGE NO BROADWAY FAN CAN RESIST! THE TEXT ABOUT THE SHOWS WAS WRITTEN BY RENOWNED BROADWAY HISTORIAN STANLEY GREEN, AND IS DRAWN FROM HIS BOOK *BROADWAY MUSICALS SHOW BY SHOW.* THIS IS DEFINITELY THE ULTIMATE COLLECTION OF BROADWAY MUSIC AND HISTORY — BE SURE TO COLLECT THE WHOLE SERIES!

BROADWAY MUSICALS SHOW BY SHOW 1940 - 1949
SHOW DESCRIPTIONS AND OVER 45 SONGS FROM THE BROADWAY HITS *PAL JOEY, OKLAHOMA!, CAROUSEL, ANNIE GET YOUR GUN, FINIAN'S RAINBOW, SOUTH PACIFIC* AND MORE. SONGS INCLUDE: ANOTHER OP'NIN, ANOTHER SHOW • BALI HAI • BEWITCHED • DIAMOND'S ARE A GIRL'S BEST FRIEND • IF I LOVED YOU • NEW YORK, NEW YORK • OH, WHAT A BEAUTIFUL MORNIN' • OLD DEVIL MOON • SOME ENCHANTED EVENING • THE SURREY WITH THE FRINGE ON TOP • YOU'LL NEVER WALK ALONE • MORE.
00311517 $14.95

BROADWAY MUSICALS SHOW BY SHOW 1950 - 1959
55 SONGS FROM SUCH CLASSICS AS *THE KING AND I, MY FAIR LADY, WEST SIDE STORY, GYPSY, THE SOUND OF MUSIC,* AND MORE. SONGS INCLUDE: DO-RE-MI • EDELWEISS • EVERYTHING'S COMING UP ROSES • GETTING TO KNOW YOU • I COULD HAVE DANCED ALL NIGHT • I'VE GROWN ACCUSTOMED TO HER FACE • LET ME ENTERTAIN YOU • LUCK BE A LADY • MACK THE KNIFE • MARIA • SEVENTY SIX TROMBONES • SHALL WE DANCE? • SOMEWHERE • WOULDN'T IT BE LOVERLY • AND MORE.
00311518 $14.95

BROADWAY MUSICALS SHOW BY SHOW 1960 - 1971
OVER 45 SONGS FROM SHOWS SUCH AS *OLIVER!, CABARET, CAMELOT, HELLO, DOLLY!, FIDDLER ON THE ROOF, JESUS CHRIST SUPERSTAR, MAME,* AND MORE. SONGS INCLUDE: AS LONG AS HE NEEDS ME • CONSIDER YOURSELF • DAY BY DAY • I DON'T KNOW HOW TO LOVE HIM • IF EVER I WOULD LEAVE YOU • IF I WERE A RICH MAN • PEOPLE • SUNRISE, SUNSET • TRY TO REMEMBER • WE NEED A LITTLE CHRISTMAS • WHAT KIND OF FOOL AM I? • AND MORE.
00311521 $14.95

BROADWAY MUSICALS SHOW BY SHOW 1972 - 1988
OVER 30 SONGS FROM THE ERA OF BIG PRODUCTIONS LIKE *PHANTOM OF THE OPERA, EVITA, LA CAGE AUX FOLLES, LES MISERABLES, ME AND MY GIRL, A CHORUS LINE, CATS* AND MORE. SONGS INCLUDE: ALL I ASK OF YOU • DON'T CRY FOR ME ARGENTINA • I AM WHAT I AM • I DREAMED A DREAM • THE LAMBETH WALK • MEMORY • THE MUSIC OF THE NIGHT • ON MY OWN • SEND IN THE CLOWNS • TOMORROW • WHAT I DID FOR LOVE • AND MORE.
00311519 $14.95

Prices, contents and availability subject to change without notice.

For more information, see your local music dealer, or write to:
Hal Leonard Publishing Corporation
P.O. Box 13819 Milwaukee, Wisconsin 53213